Words of Wisdom

Wisdom Learned is Knowledge Gained

C.J. Marie

Dedicated to my beloved family
May you find courage, wisdom and strength
to strive through life in the comfort of knowing
How much you are loved.

Love,
C.J.

Books by C. J. Marie

Words of Wisdom

Accents of a Women

Captured Thoughts

Afterthoughts of Yesterday

Legacy of Stable Dreams

Shadowed Love

Reflections of Time

Melody of Love

Days of Difference

Echoes from the Heart

Children's Stories:

Mi Primer Dia-Escolar

My First Day in Kindergarten

Chap Books:

Of Love and Sorrow

Fly With Your Dreams

Guides:

Tell Me What to Do

Pageant Tips

Introduction

During our journey of days, in each of our lives there are many sayings, quotes and trivial words that pass through our minds. Every expression often promotes feelings that can be considered to be inspirational, reflective and pleasurable.

In encouraging these various works, I have perceived them to be an awakening, a realization of truth, hidden between the confines of my mind. These thoughts generate feelings toward people, our own inhibitions and the revelation of emotion equated with each word that resonates with me. It is a gift to read a quote or phrase that has the power to stir feelings that have remained dormant and sometimes difficult to express. My comfort lies in knowing that others share the same thoughts and feelings and have expressed them so eloquently.

As we travel through the various stages of our lives we encounter many challenges. Decisions are made, consequences are faced, (Whether positive or negative) and we learn to be accountable for them while learning life's lessons. Many times, our self-worth is questioned and compromised. Yet through it all we survive with scares, wounds, and resilience. The strongest feelings of joy and hurt come from our family, our children, and love relationships. The purpose of this book is to bring peace and self-awareness to the reader. Through these selective writings which I have compiled over time, read them with openness, absorb them, internalize them and carefully see the message that will resonate with you. There is a great deal to learn about yourself if we allow the floodgates of true feelings to surface. Most likely these feelings stem back from our yesteryears and somehow our emotions are brought to the forefront of who we are today.

I will share with you a brief experience I had as a child that really was a blueprint of my life today. Coming from a very Italian traditional background and being raised by two immigrant grandparents, music was paramount in our household. I grew up with songs by Connie Frances and Mario Lanza and the like. I would sing Connie Frances songs in Italian and coming from a five-year-old little girl it was very impressive.

When visitors or family came to our home, my grandparents would dress me up, prop me up, and encourage me to perform for our guests. I couldn't sing at all but everyone loved it. I sang with so much gusto and expression it did not matter what I sounded like. Years later, I found myself performing in dance recitals, dressing up for pageants, and anything that required being center stage. Professionally, I became a teacher giving my best performance possible to educate, advocate, and motivate my students to reach for their dream. I always taught my students to never give up and to keep the vision in focus until they reach their goal.

With this being said in order to fulfill my dreams I acquired a great deal of "stuff". Many people refer to my beautiful things as "stuff". My racks of clothes, shoes, bags, jewelry, costumes, gowns, and the like have dominated my entire environment. All my awards, plaques, trophies, decorate my house. Why am I saying this? I recently came to realize that this is who I am. Every trinket, every shoe, and everything I own brings me joy. I love to dress up, I love my jewelry and all the so called "stuff" that are memories. I defend my possessions with a passion to those who encourage me to streamline. "You don't need them" they say. I have come to the new awakening that this is who I am and I do not want to live in a house that looks like a museum. I want a comfortable home filled with the memorabilia that means the world to me. I have worked hard all my life for each and every possession I have earned.

This was my epiphany. I realize that I am not giving any of this up. Not at this stage of my life. I love what I do. I respect who I am. It took more than six decades of my life to stand my ground. After collecting many of these writings in this book, I had my epiphany of freedom free of guilt. I have accepted myself for who I am and I have a right to these possessions that I deem important.

I hope these words will resonate with you and allow you to understand, accept, and live your passion and always stay true to yourself and who you really are.

Everything in your life
is a reflection of a choice you have made
if you want a different result,
make a different choice.

◆

A river cuts through a rock
not because of its power
but it's persistence.

◆

A pretty face gets old...
and a body will change...
but a good woman will always be
A good woman.

◆

As you waste your breath complaining about life
someone out there is breathing their last
appreciate what you have
be thankful and stop complaining
love more, complain less, smile more and have
less stress.

◆

Laugh your heart out
dance in the rain
cherish the moment
release the pain
live, laugh, Love
forgive and forget
Life's too short to be
living with regrets.

◆

Leave footprints of kindness
everywhere you go.

◆

Believe in yourself
and never give up on your dreams.

◆

Never let fear stand in the way
of your dreams.

◆

The greatest adventure in life
is to live your dream.
— Oprah Winfrey

Invest in what matters – YOU!

◆

*There is nothing more gratifying than
seeing the progress of a child.*

◆

*You don't stay young
doing the things of your youth
you stay young in the memories.*

◆

"A child less educated is a child most lost".
– Robert Kennedy

◆

Something truly precious holds its beauty forever.

◆

*O what a tangled web we weave
when we practice to deceive.*

◆

*Medicine heals the body
but laughter heals the soul.*

*My child and his children
are the final jewels in my crown of life.*

*Don't let the past dictate who you are
let it be who you will become.*

*If you can imagine it,
you can achieve it.
If you can dream it
you can become it.*
— Arthur Ward

*Growth is a series of mistakes.
What matters with mistakes is that we learn.*

Aging is a case of mind over matter
if you don't mind it doesn't matter.

Inspiration is the gift
we give each other.

No one could make you feel inferior
without your consent.
— Eleanor Roosevelt

"Youth is wasted on the young."
— Bernard Shaw

You can't create the future
by clinging to the past.

What makes us different
makes us unique.

The key to great happiness
is to know you can make anything out of anything.

Youth is a gift of nature
age is a work of art.

There is a fine line
between glory and disaster.

With every set back in life
there is a chance of a comeback
and a time to rise.

You can't use the past
to fill what's missing in the present.

◆

Life is a journey forever unfolding.

◆

*Each time we encounter obstacles in our life
allow them to inspire creativity.*

◆

*Elegance is not about being noticed
it's about being remembered.*

◆

Dance through the pages of your life.

◆

*Life is most fulfilling when spent
in pursuit of one's passions.*

◆

*Weave the tapestry of your life
with many diverse threads
make sure you weave the pattern
that pleases you most.*

◆

The bond between a mother and a son is a special one
it remains unchanged by time or distance
it is purest love unconditional and true
it is understanding of any situation
and forgiving of any mistakes.

Life is short
break the rules
forgive quickly,
kiss slowly,
love truly,
laugh uncontrollably,
and never regret anything
that made you smile.
—Mark Twain

◆

"Aging is not lost youth
but a new age of opportunity
and strength".
— Betty Friedman

◆

You must have courage to have glory
you must face your fears
to feel the victory.
— C.J. Marie

It is during the worst storms of your life
that you will get to see the true colors
of the people who say they care for you.

Being someone's first love
is great, but to be their last
is beyond perfect.

Don't wait until it's too late to tell someone
how much you love them, how much you care
because when they're gone,
no matter how loud you shout and cry
they won't hear you anymore.

Forgive people in your life, even those who
are not sorry for their actions.
holding on to anger only huts you
not them.

◆

If they miss you they'll call
if they want you, they'll say it.
and if not, they aren't worth your time.

◆

Life has knocked me down
a few times. It has shown me things I never
wanted to see. I have experienced sadness and failures
but one thing for sure
I always get up.

◆

The best things in life
are the people you love, places you've been,
and the memories you've made along the way.

When someone is going through a storm
your silent presence is more powerful than
a million empty words.

◆

Accept what is, let go
of what was,
and have faith in what will be.

◆

When you have a good heart
you often help too much, trust too much,
give too much, and love too much
and yet it always seems that
you're the one that hurts the most.

◆

A real woman can do it all herself
but a real man wouldn't let her.

◆

Being a mother doesn't mean
being related to someone by blood
it means loving someone unconditionally
and with your whole heart.

◆

Sometimes life is about
risking everything for a dream
that no one can see but you.

◆

The greatest source of happiness
is the ability to be grateful all the time.

◆

There is something wrong
with your character if opportunity
controls your loyalty.

◆

Don't be afraid of being different
be afraid of being the same as
everyone else.

◆

Should you find yourself a victim of other
peoples bitterness, smallness or insecurities, remember
things could be worse
you could be them.

Be a girl with a mind
a woman with attitude
and a lady with class.

"Let no man pull you
low enough to hate him".
– Martin Luther King

You can't force people to stay in your life
staying is a choice, so be thankful
for people who choose you.

How people treat other people
is a direct reflection of how
they feel about themselves.

If you stumble, make it part of the dance.

*The only way to do great work
is to love what you do.*

*Change starts with you
but it doesn't start until you do.*
— Tom Ziglar

*"The self must know stillness
before it can discover its true song."*
— Ralph Brum

*Just when the caterpillar thought the world was over
it became a butterfly.*
— Proverb

*The saddest moments are when the person who gave you
the best memories becomes a memory.*

Talking to your best friend
is sometimes all the therapy you need.

Some people are magic
and others are just the illusion of it.
— Beau Taplin

Sometimes the prettiest smiles
hide the deepest secrets.

The prettiest eyes
have cried the most tears
and the kindest hearts
have felt the most pain.

Everyone who has come into your life
is either a blessing or a lesson.

I am learning how to walk away
to walk away from people and situations
that threaten my peace of mind, self-respect or my self-worth!

Keep your friends close
and your enemies closer
the problem is you can't
tell them apart any more.

Everyone wants to be remembered
if not widely-deeply by one.
— C.J. Marie

No amount of physical beauty
will ever be as valuable as
a beautiful heart.

It's crazy how you can go months or years
without talking to someone but they
still cross your mind every day.
— Minion quotes

I am who I am,
like me, love me,
know that I am a true friend to the end
and ask for nothing in return
except two things
don't hurt me or use me...

Sometimes the person who
has been there for everyone else
needs someone to be there for them.

Keep going
everything you need
will come to you
at the perfect time.

I'm guilty of giving people more chances than they deserve,
but when I'm done I'm done.

Happiness is inside you
not in another person.

Those who love don't go away
they walk beside us every day.

Life is so much brighter
then we focus on what really matters.
A child is like a butterfly in the wind
some can fly higher than others
but each one flies as best it can.
Why compare one against the other?
Each one is different
each one is special.
Each one is beautiful
In their own way.

Every accomplishment
starts with a decision.

My greatest wish is
that my child always knows
how much I love him, and that
he walks through life knowing
I'll always be there for him anyway I can.

Remember when you forgive,
you heal.
When you let go, you grow.
In the blink of an eye
everything can change.
So forgive often and love
with all your heart.
You may never know when you may not
have that chance again.

◆

Friendship is not about
who you've known the longest.
It's about who walked into your life and said
"I'm here for you" and proved it.

◆

"Years of love have been forgot,
in the hatred of a minute."
— Edgar Allen Poe

◆

Some people dream of success
while others wake up and
work at it.

◆

*We learn something through everyone
that passes through our lives,
some lessons are painless and some are priceless.*

◆

*Having a soft heart in a cruel world
is courage not weakness.*

◆

*Cherish every moment and every person in your life,
because you never know when it will be the last
time you will see them.*

◆

*You will end up disappointed if you
think people will do for you as you do for them.
Not everyone has the same heart you do.*

◆

*"The only person you are destined to become
is the person you decide to be."*
— Ralph Waldo Emerson

◆

Love will thaw a frozen heart.

◆

Life is short spend it with friends
who make you laugh and feel loved.

◆

Just because I can handle pain
doesn't mean I deserve it.

◆

Of course size matters
no one wants a small glass of wine.

◆

A person that truly loves you will
never let you go
no matter how hard the situation is.
— Curiano.com

There are so many lessons to be learned in life. Until we see a saying or a quote do we stop and think "that's true." We think about it and then forget it. Truly absorbing it and having it resonate inwardly sometimes takes too much effort. There is always truth to quotes and worth the time to identify with them.

Everyone says time waits for no one and there is no guarantee on tomorrow. We must believe in ourselves and have strength in our faith and convictions. It is true life is an adventure and as busy as we are time passes and years go by without even noticing. Oftentimes we wonder how we even got to the place we are in.

In life there will always be setbacks and always an opportunity to come back better than ever. It's all in how we perceive things and how we choose to weave our decisions into the tapestry of our lives. Forgiveness is the ability to "let go". Letting go is crucial to inner peace, if you don't forgive, it can only hurt you in the long run.

Live in gratefulness, recognize the positives instead of the negatives. If you don't, you become a victim of bitterness. Never depend on anyone to make you happy. True happiness can only be found within yourself. Every person we come in contact within our lives teaches us something we need to learn. Some lessons are painful, and some lessons are priceless.

We have been taught to believe to treat others with kindness and understanding and in turn that will come back to us. Sometimes we quickly find that kind of thinking to be disappointing, however we need to keep in mind doing good always outweighs the negative. The decisions you make in your life mold you into the person you are today.

Family is not always blood.
It's the people in your life who want
you in theirs; the ones who accept you for who you are.
The ones who would do anything to see you
smile and love you no matter what.

◆

People don't always need advice
sometimes all they really need is a hand to hold,
an ear to listen,
and a heart to understand them.

◆

I am a teacher
I'm not in it for the income
I'm in it for the outcome.

Son I closed my eyes but a moment
and suddenly a man stood where a boy used to be.
I may not carry you now in my arms but
I will always carry you in my heart.

◆

You have given me many reasons to be proud
of the man you have become,
but the proudest moment for me is telling others
that you are my son.
I love you forever.

◆

Death leaves a heartache no one can heal,
love leaves a memory no one can steal.

◆

No matter what happens
my son comes first.

◆

A Daddy isn't defined
as the man who makes the child,
but rather a man who extends his hands
and time to raise the child
and gives his heart and love to the child!!!
Blood doesn't always make you a daddy
being a Daddy comes from the heart...
any fool can make a baby.
It takes a man to raise a child!

◆

*Good friends are like stars
you don't always see them, but you know they are there.*

◆

*I love my age.
Old enough to know better,
young enough not to care,
experienced enough to do it right.*

◆

*Journey of acceptance
from the woman I was
to the woman I have become.*

◆

*Children shouldn't have to sacrifice
so that you can have
the life you want.*

◆

The key to my heart is my child.

◆

No matter how educated, talented, rich you
believe you are, how you
treat people ultimately, tells all.
Integrity is everything.

Today will never come again.
Be a blessing.
Be a friend.
Encourage someone.
Take time to care.
Let your words heal,
and not wound.

Always smile back at a child
to ignore them is to
destroy their belief that
the world is good.

Life is too short to
worry about what people think of you.
Have fun and give them something to talk about.

In my life; I have lived, I've loved,
I've lost, I've missed, I've hurt,
I've trusted, I've made mistakes, but most of all
I've learned.
— Sun-gazing.com

◆

Seeing my child happy
is one of the best feelings in the world.
Nothing soothes the soul
like walking on the beach.

◆

All things are possible
to him who believes.
— Mark 9:23

◆

I don't know how my story will end,
but nowhere in my text will it ever read
"I gave up."

◆

Everyone makes mistakes in their life,
but that doesn't mean they have to pay for them
the rest of their life.
Sometimes good people make bad choices,
it doesn't mean they are bad.
It means they are human.

If I could give one gift in life,
I would give you the ability
to see yourself through my eyes,
only then would you realize
how special you are to me.

The past cannot be changed, forgotten
or erased; it can only be accepted.
I don't't trust words
I trust actions.

When you rest your head on a pillow
and tears start flowing subconsciously...
that's when you know you're really broken.

Your children will become what you are;
so be what you want them to be.

◆

Being a family
means you are part of something
very wonderful.
It means you will love and be loved
for the rest of your life.
No Matter what.
— Christi and Frank Bonsangue

◆

A true friendship is two imperfect people
refusing to give up on each other.

◆

I think the scariest part of being loved by someone
is the uncertainty that they may stop at any time.

◆

True friendship isn't about being inseparable;
it's being separated and nothing changes.

◆

Life is all about balance.
Be kind but don't let people abuse your
trust, but don't be deceived.
Be content, but never
stop improving yourself.

◆

As we get older we don't lose friends
we learn who the real ones are.

◆

I want to be so distracted
loving life that I never
realize I'm getting older.
— Angel Lang Sutton

Sometimes you don't realize
the weight of something
you've been carrying until
you feel the weight of its release.
— Power of Positivity

◆

...and she loved a little boy very much-
even more than she loved herself
she calls him Son.

◆

Something to think about:
At 6 yrs old – "Mommy I love you"
At 10 yrs old - "Mom, whatever"
At 16 yrs old - "Mom is so annoying"
At 18 yrs old -"I want to leave this house."
At 25 yrs old - "Mom you were right."
At 30 yrs old - "I want to go to Mom's house."
At 50 yrs old - "I don't want to lose my Mom."
At 70 yrs old - "I would give up everything for my Mom
to be here with me."

◆

I survived an Italian childhood.
– Sal Bonsangue

◆

*Beautiful things happen when
you distance yourself from negativity.
Grief never ends...but it changes.*

◆

*It's a passage, not a place to stay.
Grief is not a sign of weakness, nor a lack of faith.
It is the price of love.*

◆

*"Happiness is the best revenge,
because nothing drives your
enemies more insane than
seeing you smiling
and living a good life."*

◆

*Happiness isn't getting what you want all the time.
It's about loving what you have
and being grateful for it.*

◆

I might not be someone's first choice
but I am a great choice.
I don't pretend to be someone
I'm not, because I'm good at being me.
I might not be proud of some of the
things I've done in the past, but I am proud
of who I am today.
I may not be perfect but I don't need to be
take me as I am or watch me as I walk away.
I want to live my life without stress
or worries
I don't need to be rich or famous
I just want to be happy.

◆

Before getting upset
always ask yourself:
will this even matter in six months,
in a year, or in five years?
If the answer is no
just let it go.
– Dr. Laura

◆

There comes a time
when you have to stop crossing oceans for people
who wouldn't jump puddles for you.
– Dr. Laura

Sometimes memories sneak out of my eyes
and roll down my cheeks.

I wouldn't have to manage my anger
if people would manage their stupidity.

When you start doubting yourself.
Remember how far you have come.
Remember everything you have faced
all the battles you have won,
and all the fears you have overcome.

Until WE Meet Again
Those special memories of you
will always bring a smile, if only I
could have you back for
just a little while
then we could sit and talk again
just like we used to do.
You always meant so very much and
you always will too.
The fact that you are no longer
here will always cause me pain
but you're forever in my heart
Until we meet again.
—Zahahd Irfan

◆

Eventually all the pieces fall into place.
Until then, laugh at the confusion,
live for the moment
and know that everything happens for a reason.

◆

At your best,
you still won't be enough
for the wrong person.
At your worst,
you will still be worth it to the right person.
— Steve Maraboli.com

Nothing lasts forever, so live it up,
drink it down, laugh it off
avoid the drama, take chances, and never have regrets
because everything you did was exactly
what you wanted.
— Marilyn Monroe

We don't stop playing because we grow old.
We grow old because we stop playing.

◆

Don't understand me.
I know more than I say,
think more than I speak.
and notice more than you realize.

◆

One of the hardest lessons in life is letting go.
Whether it's guilt, anger, love, loss, or betrayal.
Change is never easy.
We fight to hold on and we fight to let go.

◆

Two things define you,
your patience when you have nothing
and your attitude when you have everything.
— BillyCox.com

◆

Life is short
cut out the negativity,
forget gossip,
say good-bye to people who hurt you.
Spend your days with the people who are always there.

◆

Sons may grow out of their toys
but in a mothers hearts of mothers they
are still their little boys.
— All great quots.com

◆

The best portion of your life will be the small,
meaningless moments you spend smiling with
someone who matters to you.

◆

One goal as a mother
is to raise children
that don't have to recover
from their childhood.

◆

Sometimes the strongest women
are the ones who love beyond all faults,
cry behind closed doors, and fights
battles that nobody knows about.
— Medwedapps.com

The best things in life
are the people we love,
the places we've seen,
and the memories we made along the way.

◆

A grandmother always thinks
about her grandchildren day and night.
Even if they are not with her, and will love them in a way
they will never understand.

◆

Every one you meet is fighting a battle
you know nothing about
be kind always.
— Robin Williams

◆

Pretending to be happy
when you're in pain
is an example of how
strong you are as a person.
— Minion quotes

◆

The best way to b happy with someone
is to learn to be happy alone.
That way the company will be a
matter of choice...
not a necessity.

◆

Never take your loved ones for granted
because you never know when their hearts will stop
beating and you won't have the chance to say good-bye.
— Fb/Best quotes empire

Getting older isn't about an end, but a beginning —
a time to fulfill old dreams and make a new reality.
So grow older with a new attitude.
— Pfizer

How old would you be
if you didn't know how old you are?
—Satchel Paige

At age 20, we worry about what others think of us.
At Age 40, we don't care about what people think of us.
At age 60, we discover they haven't been thinking of us at all.
— Ann Landers

Just remember when you're over the hill
you begin to pick up speed.
— Charles M. Schulz

◆

The best therapy in the world
is time out with your friends.

◆

It's not what happens in your life that matters.
It's how you respond to what happens to you
that makes a difference.
— Zig Ziglar

◆

"Those who are the hardest to love...
need it the most. "

◆

If you can't make sacrifices for your children
you don't deserve to have them.
There are so many adults that would
love to be able to have children and can't.
Having children is a privilege not a right!
Give your child the life they truly deserve!

◆

The best thing in life
is finding someone
who knows all your faults, mistakes,
and weaknesses and still thinks
you're completely amazing.

Be thankful for what you have,
you will end up having more.
If you concentrate on what you don't have,
you'll never have enough.
— Oprah Winfrey

I have never met a strong person
with an easy past.

Life is so ironic.
It takes sadness to know happiness
noise to appreciate silence,
and absence to value presence.

Sometimes you will never know
the value of a moment
until it becomes a memory.
— Dr Suess

Suicide doesn't take away the pain,
it gives it to someone else.

It's not what we have in life,
but who we have in our life
that matter.

My entire life can be described in one sentence:
it didn't go as planned, and that's OK.

God sometimes removes people from your life
to protect you.
Don't run after them.

*"I think the saddest people always try their hardest
to make people happy.
Because they know what it's like to feel
absolutely worthless and they don't want
anyone else to feel like that. "*
— Robin Williams
Fb/David Arnardo Wolfe

*Honesty has power
that very few people can handle.*

*I forgive you, but I also learn a lesson.
I won't hate you, but I will never get close
enough for you to hurt me again.
I can't let forgiveness become foolishness.*
— Tony Gaskens

*Forgive yourself for the blindness
that put you in the blindness
that put you in the path of those who betrayed you.
Sometimes a good heart doesn't see the bad.*
— Darty carma quotes.com

I adore his smile
I cherish his hugs
I admire his heart
But most of all...
I love that he is
MY SON.

I've always loved butterflies, because they remind us
that it's never too late to transform ourselves.

My child is my heart and soul
He will always be my baby.
Even when he grows old.
— Drew Barymore

When thinking about life
remember this:
No amount of guilt can solve the past
and no amount of anxiety can change the future.

We never know
how strong we are
until we are tested.
— C.J. Marie

Integrity is choosing your thoughts and actions
based on values rather than personal gain.
—Montarano website

Instead of complaining, ask God
"What are you trying to teach me."

Simple things become complicated
when you expect to much.

Everything in life is easier
when you don't concern yourself
with what everyone else is doing.
— Hplyrlk.com

Never put the key to your happiness
in someone else's pocket.
— Ku Shandwizdon

Inhale the future,
exhale the past.

Honesty is a very expensive gift,
don't expect it from cheap people.
— Husband wisdom

If you're not helping to make it right,
then stop complaining about
it being wrong...

Someone who loves you
wouldn't put themselves
in a position to lose you.
— Trentshelton

*The fact that you
are not where you want to be
should be enough motivation to get you there.*

*Never chase love, affection or attention.
If it isen't given freely by another person
it isen't worth having.*

*Be a reflection of what you want to receive.
If you want love, give love.
If you want truth, be truthful.
What you give out will always return.*

*The greatest prison people live in
is the fear of what others people think.*

*Almost every successful person begins with two beliefs:
the future can be better than the present,
and I have the power to make it so.*

The best thing I ever did
was to believe in myself.

Luck is what happens
when preparation meets opportunity.

Be careful who you open up to.
Only a few people actually care,
the rest just want something
to gossip about.

Don't talk,
act.
Don't say,
do.
Don't promise
prove.

Behind every successful person
there is a lot of unsuccessful years.

Sometimes we create our own heartbreaks
through expectations.

Pay attention to people who don't' clap when you win.

If you are persistent, you will get it.
If you are consistent, you will keep it.

Surround yourself with people
that reflect who you want to be
and how you want to feel,
energies are contagious.

In the end you will see
who's fake,
who's true
and would risk it all for you.

Rejection doesn't mean you aren't good enough,
it means that other people failed to notice
what you have to offer.
— Mark Amend

"If you want to be original.
be ready to be copied. "
— CoCo Chanel

Never allow yourself to be defined
by someone else's opinion of you.

I'm stronger because I had to be.
I had to be smarter
because of my mistakes.
Happier because of the sadness I've known
and now wiser because I learned.

Worrying does not take away tomorrow troubles,
it takes away today's peace.

Things money can't buy:
Manners
Morals
Respect
Character
Common sense
Trust

A bad attitude is like a flat tire
you can't go anywhere
until you change it.

It's better to know and be disappointed
than to never know and always wonder.
— Extramadness,com

A persons' action will tell you
everything you need to know.

Your only obligation in any lifetime
is to be true to yourself.

Often we can look back at our past and just reminisce or we can dwell on the memories and get stuck in a time warp. Should of, could of, would of, have no place in the present. Leave yesterday behind and move forward. It's a nice feeling to go back to the good old days but things have changed, and we have grown into the world of today. Happy or sad thoughts are best left behind in order to move forward with hope.

As decades of time pass you realize the family you had in your childhood days are gone forever. Be grateful for the time you shared being together and the memories you made. Just remember to love those who are around you now and stay distant from those individuals who are toxic in your life.

I strongly believe that everything happens for a reason. Those who come into our lives are there for a purpose we just have to have the awareness to see it. Time will pass, we get old, and the cycle of life continues. Memories are our treasures that live in our heart. Life is meant to be lived today and not in the past.

*The past is a place of reference
not a place of residence.*

*Discipline is the one thing necessary
to achieve any goal worth having.
Sometimes the most important thing
you'll need to know
is how to be your own best friend.
The goodrule.com*

*The secret of getting ahead
is getting started.*

*Be strong enough to stand alone,
smart enough to know when you need help
and brave enough to ask for it.*

*You were born to be real
not perfect.*

*Most of the problems in life are because
of two reasons, we act without thinking
or we keep thinking without acting.*

*The closer you get to excellence in your life,
the more friends you lose.
When your just average it makes people more comfortable,
but when you pursue greatness
it makes people uncomfortable.
Be prepared to lose some people on your journey.*
— Tony A. Gaskin Jr.

*Being told your appreciated
is one of the simplest yet incredible
uplifting things you can ever hear.*

*Surround yourself with the dreamers and the doers,
the believers and the thinkers, but most of
all surround yourself with those who see the
greatness within you
even when you don't see it yourself.*

Sometimes you have to do what is best
for you and your life,
not what is best for everyone else.
— Iliketoquote.com

It is during the worst times of your life
that you will get to see the true colors
of the people who say they care for you.

Every champion was a contender
that refused to give up.

People who have no life
will always start drama in yours.

Ambition doesn't take a vacation.

You have to be brave to live
the truth of who you are.
— C.J. Marie

"Loving someone is giving them the power
To break your heart,
but trusting them not to. "
— Julianne Moore

I don't belong where I'm not wanted.

The bond between grandchildren and their grandparents
Is one that is so strong.
It can never be broken.
They hold each other's hearts forever.

My grandchildren are my legacy.
— C.J. Marie

If you don't laugh in life, you cry.
play your life out on the world stage.

Imagine yourself with no limitations...
only potential.

*True friends are those rare people who come
to find you in dark places
and lead you back to the light.*
— Womenworking.com

*Some of the best advice you'll ever get will
come from listening to your instincts.*
— Live life happily.com

*"All it takes is a beautiful fake smile to hide an injured soul
and they will never notice how broken you are."*
— Robin Williams

*"Carry out a random act of kindness
with no expectation of reward,
safe in the knowledge that one day
someone might do the same for you."*
— Princess Diana

*Every accomplishment
begins with a decision to try.*

As I grew older I thought
the best part of my life was over
then I was handed my grandchild
and realized the best part of my life
had just begun.

As I unclutter my life
I free myself to answer
the calling of my soul.

It takes one song
to bring back a thousand memories.

Sometime you have to just accept the fact
that certain things will never go back to how
they used to be.

My childhood family is gone forever.

A dream starts with a vision.
Perseverance and dedication
turns the dream into reality.

◆

"The greatest adventure in life
Is to live your dream."
— Oprah

◆

I wish more people would understand
just how much their words and
actions affect others.

The old are wise
the young are fearless.

If you're feeling a little down,
remember some of the best days in your life
haven't happened yet.
— Steven Aitchison

◆

*Make choices
not excuse.*

◆

*Dance while you can,
enjoy while you can.
Time waits for no one
and it is all we have.*

◆

*Beauty isn't about having a pretty face.
It's about having a pretty mind, a kind heart,
and most importantly a beautiful soul.*

◆

*A tear is made up of 1% water
and 90% of feelings.*

◆

*Someday your future
will be your past.*

◆

If you don't know where you are going
you will end up somewhere else.
— Yogi Berra

Forgive people in your life,
even those who are not sorry for their actions.
Holding on to anger only hurts you
not them.

Glam-ma- a noun
A woman whose children have had children
but she is far too glamorous to be called grandma.

Never apologize for how much love you have to give.
Just feel sorry for those who didn't
want any of it.

No one notices your tears
no one notices your sadness
no one notices your pains
but everyone notices your mistakes.

I may not be perfect
but when I look at my child
I know that I did something perfectly right.

◆

Growth is painful
change is painful
but nothing is as painful
as being somewhere you don't belong.

◆

Loyalty is about people who stay true to you
behind your back.

◆

Common sense is not a gift it is a punishment
because you have to deal with everyone
who doesn't have it.

◆

Don't ever stray away from yourself
to get closer to someone else.

◆

Travel while you're young and able
don't worry about the money,
just make it work.
Experience is far more valuable
than money will ever be.

The best feeling in the world
is knowing that you actually
mean something to someone.

Life is too short
to wake up in the morning with regrets.
So love the people who treat you right.
Forgive those who don't
and believe everything happens for a reason.

A negative mind will never give you
a positive life.

Life is too short to put up with fools.

Walk away from anything or anyone
who takes away from your joy.
A perfect marriage is two imperfect people
who refuse to give up on each other.

The biggest lie I tell myself is:
"I don't need to write it down,
I'll remember it."
— Minion quotes

It is not what you do for your children,
but what you have taught them to do for themselves,
that will make them successful human beings.
— Ann Landers

Good friends help you to find important things
when you have lost them...
your smile, your hope, and your courage.
— Doe Zantomata

Everybody who has gone through something
that has changed them in such a way that they never
could go back to the person they once were.

Let your children know you support them
regardless of their performance.

Death leaves a heartache
no one can heal...
but love leaves a memory
no one can steal.

Miracles happen every day.
Change your perspective of what a miracle is
and you'll see them all around you.
— Jon Bon Jovie

Don't let anyone ever dull your sparkle.

Be kind,
be thoughtful,
be genuine
but most of all
be thankful.

◆

When I get old I don't want people to think
"What a sweet little old lady...
I want them to say
"OH crap! What is she up to now?"

◆

When you judge another person
you do not define them;
you define yourself.
— Wayne Dyer

◆

You may see me struggle
but you will never see
me give up.

◆

Breaking someone's trust
is like crumbling up a perfect
piece of paper.
you smooth it over
but it's never going to be the same.

Take me or leave me
accept me or hate me
but don't make me feel less of a person
if I don't fit your idea of who I should be.
I am me and I love me as I am.

The hardest thing a parent is watching
a child goes through
something really tough
and not being able to fix it for them.

◆

"Like the sun we are attracted to people
who shine with warmth and brightness."

◆

*"You don't inspire
your team mates by showing them
how amazing you are.
You inspire them by showing them
how amazing they are.
A head full of fears
has no space for dreams.*
— Aristotle

◆

*Life is too short to argue
and fight with the past.
Count your blessings,
value your loved ones,
and move on with
your head held high.*

◆

*In the end people will judge you anyway,
so don't live your life impressing others.
Live your life
impressing yourself.*

◆

No day shall erase you from
the memory of time.
— Virgil
In 911 memorial

I want to inspire people.
I want someone to look at me and say
"Because of you, I didn't give up".

Life isn't meant to be easy, it's meant to be lived
sometimes happy,
other times rough...
but with every up and down you learn.
Lessons that make you STRONG.

As you grow older
your Christmas list gets smaller
and the things you really want
can't be bought.

I'm called PaPa
because I'm too cool to be called
grandfather.

◆

There's nothing like a grandchild
to put a smile on your face,
a lump in your throat
and a warm feeling in your heart.

◆

Find your very own voice
and sing your heart song...

◆

Everyone in your life is meant
to be part of the journey
but not all of them are meant to stay.

◆

Be selective in your battles
sometimes peace is better than being right.

◆

There are moments in life when you miss
someone so much
that you just want to pick them out from
your dreams and hug them for real.

Life is like a camera
focus on what's important
capture the good times
develop from the negative
and if things don't work out
take another shot.

◆

Your hardest time
often leads to the
greatest moments of your life.
Keep the faith.
It will be worth it in the end.

I will never forget the neighborhood
or the friends I grew up with
or the great times we had.

◆

*Perhaps they are not stars
in the sky but rather
openings where our loved ones shine down
to let us know they are happy.*

*Grace is when somebody hurts you
and you try to understand their situation
instead of trying to hurt them back.*

*There are some people who always seem angry
and continuously look for conflict.
Walk away; the battle they are fighting isn't with you,
it is with themselves.*

*The only people I owe loyalty to
are those that never made
me question theirs.*

*The moment you created another human being,
was the moment you chose to spend
the rest of your life putting somebody else first.*

"I admire people who choose to shine even after
all the storms they've been through.

◆

Too often we underestimate the power of touch,
a smile, a kind word,
a listening ear,
an honest compliment,
or the smallest act of caring, all of which
have the potential to turn a life around.

◆

I am not in any competition with anyone.
I have no desire to play the game of being better
Than anyone.
I am simply trying to be a better person
than I was yesterday.

◆

No matter how badly people treat you,
never drop down to their level,
just know you are better and walk away.

◆

This year is almost gone.
Not all our friends and family made it.
Never take for granted the people you love.

◆

Slow down and enjoy the journey right now.
Take time for the people in your life
they won't always be there.

◆

Inside every older person
is a younger person wondering
what the hell happened.
– Cora Harvey Armstrong

◆

I don't want my child to follow in my footsteps
I want them to take the path next to me
and go further than I could have ever dreamed possible.

The most precious jewels
you'll ever have around your neck
are the arms of your child.

Good friends care for each other,
close friends understand each other,
but true friends stay forever...beyond words,
beyond distance, beyond time.
— Christine Ward Colby

A good life is when you assume nothing,
do more, needless,
smile often, dream big,
laugh a lot and realize how blessed you are.

Have you ever stopped and realized
that if you hadn't met a certain person
your entire life could be
completely different.

Keep calm and be crazy
laugh, love, and live it up,
because this is the oldest you've been
and the youngest you'll ever be again.
— American Hippie

Karma
No need for revenge.
Just sit back and wait
those who hurt you
will eventually screw up themselves.
And if you're lucky God will let you watch.

Pretending to be happy
When you're in pain
is just an example of
how strong you really are
as a person.

No expectations
Less disappointments.

◆

When you love someone so much,
you can still hear their voice and laughter
after they're gone.
– Healing Hugs

◆

There is magic in simplicity and beauty in every day. How many of us stop and think about how great simple things in life are? For example: taking that first sip of coffee in the morning and smelling the aroma of freshly toasted bread or just sitting in the sunshine near a window on a cold winter's day. There are so many magical moments around us that are taken for granted with each waking minute. Sitting by a fireplace sipping wine or tea enjoying the comfort of your home and the warmth your own special time.

There are a multitude of reflections to ponder that call us to witness the beauty life has to offer. All that is required is to be mindful and appreciate simplicity and heed the moment of enjoyment.

*"You can never completely know anyone,
no matter how well you think you do,
there will always be some truth about them
you never get to know. "*
— Susan Colasanti

◆

*A strong person is not the one who doesn't cry.
A strong person is one who is quiet and sheds tears
for a moment, and then picks up her sword and fights again.*

◆

*A step parent is so much more than just a parent.
They made the choice to love when they didn't have to.*

◆

*If you don't leave your past in the past,
it will destroy your future.
Live for what today has to offer,
not for what yesterday has taken away.*

◆

When you lose someone we love,
we must learn not to live without them...
but to live with the love they left behind.
— Healing hugs

Life is too short
to waste a single second
with anyone who doesn't value you.

"Students who are loved at home
come to school to learn.
And students who don't
come to school to be loved.
—Nicholas A. Ferrioni

Remember the smallest light
shines the brightest
for someone in darkness.

Some days I wish I could I could go back in life,
not to change things,
just to feel a few things twice.

Life only comes around once,
so do whatever makes you happy,
and be with whoever makes you smile.
(daily karma quotes)

The challenge of the search
enhances the thrill of the find.

I've come to realize that the only people I need in my life
are the ones who need me in theirs,
even when I have nothing else to offer them but myself.

♦

Wrinkles mean you laughed,
gray hair means you cared,
and scares mean you lived.

♦

When you stop chasing the wrong things
you give the right things
a chance to catch up.

I've never met a strong person
with an easy past.

Be careful who you vent to
a listening ear is also
a running mouth.

Sometimes the people who are
a thousand miles away from you,
can make you feel better than those people
standing beside you.

It is easier to build strong children
than to repair broken adults.
— Frederick Douglas

"Be more concerned with your character
than your reputation
because your character is what you really are,
while your reputation is merely what others think of you. "
— John Wooden

Nothing is sexier
than a man who can face temptation
and have the level of maturity
to say this isn't worth
losing what I have.

In a blink of an eye,
everything can change.
So forgive often love with all your heart,
you may never have that chance again.

"I love the person I have become,
because I fought to become her. "
— Kate Diane

You can change direction
by just thinking about it.

The only things you can take with you in this world
are the things you've packed inside your heart.
— Susan Gal

We are the choices we make
and choices is what creates your life.

People hate it when you show them
how it feels to be treated the way they treat you.

Not everyone likes me
but not everyone matters...

◆

You can be bitter or better,
pitiful or powerful,
but you can't be both
— Joyce Meyer

◆

The happiest people don't have the best of everything
they just make the best of everything they have.

◆

Life is measured in moments
make the most of them.

◆

A good life is when you assume nothing,
do more, need less,
smile often, dream big,
laugh often, and realize
how blessed you are.

◆

Always tell someone, how you feel
because opportunities are lost
in the blink of an eye
and regrets can last a lifetime.
No matter what people think of you,
always keep singing your own song.

◆

*Sometimes I wish I could
just rewind back to the old days
and press pause...
just for a little while.*

*You have become, but
the proudest moment
for me is telling others
that you are my son.
I love you now and forever.*

*If you can't be positive
then at least be quiet.*
— Joel Olsteen

Remember no one is perfect and we all have flaws. Be open to forgiveness if someone has done you wrong. There are no perfect parents, no perfect children, no perfect friend or spouse. We all have our own imperfections. I choose to believe there is good in everyone even if at times it is clouded with irate behavior. There is a definite lack of tolerance in our world today and anger seems to have taken center stage.

We need to rise above this anger, accept what we cannot change and understand many people today are not on an even keel of life. No matter how difficult it is, just move on. The world is filled with unbalanced individuals trying to cope with the stresses of their lives. We all have imperfections, we are clearly a work in progress and that is what makes each of us individually extraordinary.

Don't regret getting old
It's a privilege denied to many.

Week seek people revenge
strong people forgive.
Intelligent people ignore.

The less you respond to negative people,
the more peaceful
your life will become.

Believe in yourself
and all that you are.
know that there is
something inside you
that is greater than any obstacle.
— Hugs & Kisses

If you truly love someone
being faithful is easy.

Be kind, you never know
the invisible hurts others
might be carrying.
Don't lose hope...
sometimes the greatest triumphs come from
the deepest challenges.
— Jane Lee Logan

Focus on what you have
instead on what you don't have.
On what's right in the world
instead of what's wrong.
On where you are going
instead of what you've been through.
— Billy Cox

Enjoy the little things in life.
for one day you will look back
and realize they were the big things.

*"If you hear people from the past speak of me
keep in mind they are speaking of a person
they don't even know anymore."*

*It's easier to fake a smile
than to explain why your sad.*

*Today I close the door to the past,
open the door to the future,
take a deep breath step on through
and start a new chapter in my life.*

*Once you feel you are avoided by someone
never disturb them again.*

*My greatest gift is that my grandchildren
always know how much I love them.*

◆

*The saddest thing about betrayal
it never comes from an enemy.*

◆

Life is a journey not a destination
it is during the journey
that lessons are learned, memories are made
and the strength to succeed is found.

◆

Hold him a little closer
rock him a little more
tell him another story
(You only told him four)
let him sleep on your shoulder
rejoice in his happy smile
he is only a little boy
for such a little while.

◆

If you're looking for that one person
that will change your life
look in the mirror.

◆

"There are no perfect parents
and there are no perfect children,
but there are plenty of perfect moments.
– DaveWillis.org

◆

I choose to live by choice not by chance;
to make changes, not excuses;
to be motivated not manipulated;
to be useful, not used;
to excel, not compete
I choose self-esteem; not self-pity
I choose to listen to my inner voice;
not the random opinion of others.

◆

Family
Like branches on a tree
we all grow in different directions
but our roots remain the same.

◆

A real woman can do it all herself.
but a real man wouldn't let her.

◆

You cannot change the people around you,
but you can change the people you choose
to be around.

◆

Don't wait for things to get easier, simpler, better.
Life will always be complicated.
Learn to be happy right now.
Otherwise you'll run out of time.

"There is no substitute for victory."
— General Douglas MacArthur

Every decision made and actions we take
is a statement of exactly how much we are valuing ourselves.
Be kind to yourself.
— Lynda Field

Don't forget to strut your
inner tiara today.
— Janie Lee Logan

◆

The fault lies not in our stars
but in ourselves.
— Shakespeare, *Julius Caesar*

◆

I may not be perfect,
but when I look at my child
I know I must have gotten something right.

A mother thinks of her children day and night
even if they are not with her, she will love them in a way
they will never understand.

Children need to learn to take responsibility for their actions
so that they do not become adults believing that
nothing is ever their fault.

Be with someone
who always wants to know
how your day was.

A good laugh and a long sleep
are the two best cures for anything.
– Irish proverb

*I just need someone to hug me and tell me
I'm not as worthless as I think I am.*

*You can learn great things from your mistakes
when you are not busy denying them.*

*People will come and go in your life
but the right ones will always stay.*

*Just being there for someone can sometimes
bring hope when all seems hopeless.*
— Dave G. Llewellyn

*I am to positive to be doubtful,
to optimistic to be fearful and
to determine to be defeated.*

*In the end we only regret
the chances we didn't take.*

Do not shrink your beautiful light
to make someone else feel more comfortable.
Be who you are without hesitation and
you will inspire others to shine, too.

◆

I am not the most important person in your life...
I just hope that when you hear my name...
you smile and say that's my friend.

◆

We don't meet people by accident.
They are meant to cross our path for a reason.

◆

You'll be his first kiss,
his first love,
his first friend.
You are his mother and
and he is your whole world.
He's your little boy even when
he is all grown up.

◆

*"Once you have lived in New York
and made it your home,
no place is good enough, "*
— John Steinbeck

*Associate yourself with people of good quality
for it is better to be alone
than in bad company.*
— Booker T. Washington

*You are never too old to set another goal
or to dream another dream.*

*When they placed you in my arms
You slipped into my heart.
I never knew how much a person could love
until I became a mom.*
— Mothersquotes.com

I am thankful for all those difficult people
in my life.
They have shown me exactly who
I do not want to be.

◆

One day you will be at the place
you always wanted to be.

◆

Our feelings quietly depicted in a serial way.
Like words are not always simple to define
but the journey to wholeness is the challenge of life.

◆

If you've never had a mother or a father,
you grow up seeking something
you're never going to find, ever.
You seek it in love and in people and in beauty.
— "Nothing Left Unsaid" Documentary

◆

Safe means consistency of condition.

◆

"A fatherless girl thinks all things are possible
and nothing is safe." That is the core of my mom's existence.
And I always see the slight melancholy, slight sadness.
Like a shadow passing by in her eyes. "
— Anderson Cooper about Gloria Vanderbilt in
The "Nothing Left Unsaid" Documentary

"When the train meets the station
get on board. "

I love hearing old songs I used to love.
They are like memories you can always go back to.

Storms make trees take deeper roots.
— Dolly Parton

The sooner you step away from your comfort zone,
the sooner you'll realize that
really wasn't all that comfortable.
— Eddie Harris Jr.

Everything you do is based on the choices you make.
It's not your parents, your past, your relationships,
our job, the economy, the weather, an argument or
Your age that is to blame.
You and only you are responsible for every
decision and choice you make.

Knowing when to walk away is wisdom.
Being able to is courage.
Walking away, with your
held up high, is dignity.

Karma
Think good thoughts
say nice things,
do good for others.
Everything comes back.
The saddest thing about betrayal
is that it never comes from your enemies.

*Sometimes you just have to hang on
and trust that life's storms are carrying
you to better pathways.*
— Jane Lee Logan

◆

*I am truly grateful for those who stick by me
even when times are rough;
and especially when I am difficult to be around...
I cherish each and every one of you
when someone loves you they don't have to say it.
You can tell by the way they treat you.*

◆

*You either get bitter or you get better.
It's that simple, you either take
what has been dealt to you and
allow it to make you a better person,
or allow it to tear you down.
The choice does not belong to fate; it belongs to you.*
— Josh Skipp

◆

Sometimes it feels so good to just sit by yourself
relax and not talk to anyone.
— Kristen Butler

There is nothing more contagious
than the laughter of young children;
it doesn't even matter what they are a laughing about.
— Criss Jami

Sometimes it's not the song that makes you emotional
it's the people and things that come to mind when you hear it.

Sometimes quiet people really do have a lot to say
they're just being careful about who they open up to.

◆

The beach is the only place where salt
lowers your blood pressure.

◆

Every time you get upset at something,
ask yourself if you were to die tomorrow,
was it worth wasting your time being angry.
— Robert Tai

♦

Your children will become who you are;
So be who you want them to be.

♦

"Sometimes the bad things that happen in our lives
put us directly on the path to the best things
that ever happened to us."

♦

Spend time with your parents
treat them well.
because one day when you look up
from your phone, they won't be there anymore.

Whisper I love you to a butterfly
and it will fly to heaven to deliver your message.

"Ability is what your capable of doing,
motivation determines what you do,
attitude determines how well you do it."

◆

One day you'll be just a memory to some people.
Do your bests to be a good one.

◆

Sometimes the best thing you can do is not think,
not wonder, not imagine, not abscess.
Just breathe,
and have faith that everything will work out for the best.

◆

Not everyone will appreciate what you do for them.
You have to figure out who's worth your kindness
and who's just taking advantage.

◆

Two things you never have to chase,
true friends and true love.

◆

*One day I will be a crazy old lady covered in glitter
and it will be fabulous.*

◆

*A good life is when you assume nothing,
do more, need less,
smile often,
dream big,
laugh a lot,
and really know how blessed you are.*

◆

*Faith is seeing light with your heart
When all your eyes see is darkness.*

◆

*One of the hardest decisions you'll ever face in life
is choosing whether to walk away or try harder.*

◆

*Never be defined by your past.
It was just a lesson not a life sentence.*

◆

If the words you speak appeared on your skin,
would you still be beautiful?

There comes a day when turning the page
is the best decision for you
because you realize there's so much more to the book
than the page your stuck on.

None of us are getting out of this life alive,
so please stop treating
yourself like an afterthought.
Eat the delicious food, walk in the sunshine,
jump in the ocean,
say the truth that you are carrying in your heart
like a hidden treasure.
Be silly, be kind, be weird.
There's no time for anything else.
— Richard Gere

That's the problem with always putting others first;
you've taught them you come second.

Should you ever find yourself the victim
of other people's bitterness, smallness,
insecurities, remember things could be worse
you could be them.

Trust takes years to build,
seconds to break
and forever to repair.

Once you bring children into this world
it's not about you anymore.

You were wild once don't let them tame you.

A crown is made up of more than
rhinestone and gems
it's made up of courage.

Instead of hating someone
act as if their dead
it saves energy.

A child who is always disrespectful to their parents
will not have true respect for anyone.
— Rev Billy Graham

When you're mad at someone you love,
be careful what you say
because your mind gets angry
but you heart still cares.

Never give in
never give up
Never give up on your dreams
and never give up on yourself.

Passion is the fuel for success

A passion for excellence
is the gateway to success.

Memories are life's precious gifts.

It is easier to beg for forgiveness
than ask for permission.

I am not apologizing for being me.
– Dr. David Mazza

I am who I am
not who you think I am.
not who you want me to be.
I am me.
– Brigitte Nicole

It is wise to think age is a privilege with each passing year. As we listen to music of our time the feelings become invasive and bittersweet. It takes us back to another time and place of our youth or just a different time filled with memories. It is good to visit old times and treasured thoughts of the past but more important to move on. Long ago feelings tend to linger, and we must remind ourselves that it was another space in time and this is now.

We are not the same person we were back then and most likely will never be again. Life changes and not even time can define who we are. Life isn't a dress rehearsal you don't' get a second chance, and just like that it can be over. Feel free to say "I love you" to all those close to you today and don't wait until tomorrow. Be thankful for who you are and the blessings that surround you today.

No matter how old I get
I will always be young at heart.
— Brigitte Nicole

◆

Don't come to my funeral and cry over me
If you didn't care about me when you had the chance.

◆

My son is my baby today,
tomorrow and always.
You hurt him I will hurt you.
I don't care if he is 1 or 50 years old.
I will defend him and protect him all of my life.

◆

Today be thankful and remember
how rich you are:
your family is priceless,
your time is gold,
and your health is wealth.

◆

The devil doesn't come to you
with his red face and horns.
He comes to you disguised
as everything you ever wanted.

There are moments in life
when you wish you could bring someone
down from heaven, spend the day with them
just one more time, give them one more hug,
kiss them good-by or hear their voice again.
One more chance to say I love you.

Some days I wish I could go back in life.
Not to change anything,
but to feel a few things twice.

Accept what is
let go of what was
and have faith in what will be.

*The worst feeling isn't being lonely
it's being forgotten.*

*Just because I didn't react
doesn't mean I didn't notice.*

*A scare simply means you were stronger
than whatever tried to hurt you.*

*Crying is a way your eyes speak
when your mouth can't explain
how broken your heart is.*

*We are all visitors to this time,
this place.
We are just passing through.
Our purpose here is
to observe, to learn, to grow,
to love, and then we return home.*

I won't be less than my best.

◆

"I don't believe in age
I believe in energy.
Don't let age dictate what
you can and cannot do. "
— Tao Porchon-Lynch
97 years old yoga teacher

◆

A heart is not judged by how much you love;
but by how much you are loved by others.
— The Wizard of Oz

◆

Every one you meet
has something valuable to teach you.

◆

I thought growing old would take longer.

◆

The sad part of growing old
is that no one can see you're still young
on the inside.

◆

When the day arrives that there are no more tomorrows
I want my child to know and never forget that
he is and always will be deeply loved by me.

◆

Wisdom learned is
knowledge gained.
— C.J. Marie

◆

Every exit
is an entrance to somewhere else.
— Tom Stoppard

◆

Final Thoughts

Life is a precious gift in spite of its ups and down twists and turns. During difficult times it is easy for us to think otherwise. Wisdom in words can transform thoughts, attitude and ideas. Simple quotes or sayings can bring about deep feelings and generate change.

My hope is that these words will help you find true meaning and clarification in your search of self, and celebrate the wisdom you have gained through the years.

As I comprised this book my own life gained perspective and I am eager to share my thoughts and feelings with you. Inner peace comes through understanding who you are, and why you have the feelings you have. One thing is for certain stay true to yourself and always find something to be thankful for during your journey of days we call "life."

Always,

C.J. Marie